REM

REMREMREMREMREMREM

EMREM CARLTON **David Harrington**

THIS IS A CARLTON BOOK

ISBN 1 85868 207 X

Printed in Italy

THE AUTHOR

David Harrington has written for several music and lifestyle magazines in the UK, Europe and the US in the past five years. He lives and works in West London, surrounded by an ancient Amstrad and the complete works of Steely Dan.

CONTENTS

INTRODUCTION

It is the Spring of 1991. On MTV a new video is growing in the public consciousness—blossoming, blooming, exploding across the network. It is a relentlessly cheerful song, dressed up in weird images and delivered with almost manic good humour. At first it's difficult to work out exactly what's going on. Two mechanical monkeys are beating a pair of drums, an old man is pedalling away on a stationary bicycle... and then comes a sudden splash of colour, the sound of orchestral strings and one of the goofiest melodies in the history of rock music. Compared to most of MTV's routine fodder, the video for R.E.M.'s 'Shiny Happy People' is something of a revelation. Falling into the dangerous bracket of being something you either love or hate, the song and the video are impossible to ignore.

Leading the visual mayhem is a pencil-thin figure clad in a mustard-coloured jacket, shirt and bright yellow baseball cap—worn backwards, of course. Miming the song as well as he can, R.E.M.'s lead singer Michael Stipe has a constant smile playing behind his lips as his arms flail, his feet tap and a cast of video extras (including a gyrating Kate Pierson of cult-kitsch popsters the B-52s) go into a mass dance routine alongside him.

Behind Stipe stands bassist Mike Mills, studious and bespectacled, plucking at an upright bass and looking like a schoolteacher moonlighting in a rock video; the smile flickering about his face indicating a curious mixture of acute embarrassment and immense enjoyment.

To Mills' left is drummer Bill Berry, beating on a single drum with exaggerated precision while pointing at the camera, dancing awkwardly and flashing the occasional self-mocking grin from beneath the most formidable eyebrows in the history of music.

And somewhere, often off-camera, clad in a sober white shirt and black jacket, is guitarist Peter Buck. Looking heavier these days and with newly grown curtains of dark hair framing his features, he pretends to pick out the notes on a mandolin while giving the impression that he'd rather be anywhere else than stood there in another rock video...

"My earliest memory as a child was when I was two years old and had scarlet fever. I was hallucinating and I was having my picture taken. I had a sweater and I was really miserable and there was this guy zooming in and out."

Michael Stipe

Unlikely heroes

In a business that has given us the strutting, human dynamo that is Mick Jagger, the diminutive posturing of Prince and the sex siren persona of Madonna—R.E.M.'s image trails a long way behind. Four of rock'n'roll's unlikeliest stars, they have a look straight out of a marketing man's nightmare, unlike anything rock'n'roll has ever produced before—or is likely to do again. The band seem to float above the collective hype and hysteria as complete individuals, united in their collective ability to make wonderful music. Indeed they don't seem to have an 'image' as such, yet still manage to exude the same aura that more conventionally glamorous rock bands project, and they remain rock'n'roll's greatest enigma—reluctant superstars unable to quell the fanaticism of their fans or halt the media's quest to know everything about R.E.M..

And that is a lengthy quest, stretching back to a time when each band member switched on the radio and first heard heard the Beatles, the Rolling Stones, Velvet Underground and, eventually, the Sex Pistols...

TALK ABOUT THE PASSION

Considering the ambiguity and exaggeration which has perennially surrounded the early days of R.E.M. members, it's not surprising to find that their singer has been evasive about his musical background.

Recent interviews revealed that his great grandmother was an opera singer and that his father played the violin. Stipe, however, has pleaded ignorance when it comes to some of rock'n'roll's greatest names, claiming that his entire musical knowledge was gleaned from the Elvis Presley, country and western and gospel records that made up his parents' record collection.

Michael Stipe—rock'n'roll to the rescue

He was born John Michael Stipe on January 4, 1960 in the town of Decatur, Georgia, and has since referred to himself as an "army brat"; his father's military career having taken the family to homes in Georgia, Texas, Germany and Illinois. And he was

Michael Stipe

"I just sat around reading or listening to music. That year alone, I think I matured about five years… It's a long time to go without talking to people, and it really put a lot of things into perspective for me."
Michael Stipe

unusual from an early age. If rumour is to be believed, the left-handed Michael Stipe had a tendency to write backwards, in almost perfect mirror image, until his distraught teachers finally persuaded him to stop at the age of 12.

In 1975 the Stipe family moved to Collinsville, Illinois, where Michael assumed the role of the shy, bespectacled nerd in a high school full of loud, outgoing football players and rabid heavy metal fans. "I was afraid of a lot of things," he confessed later. But by the age of 15 he had become interested in rock music and was picking up on the first rumblings of punk via the imports section of the local record store

Michael Stipe—'I was afraid of a lot of things.'

and the pages of the Village Voice, the New York arts and music magazine to which he now subscribed.

At this time New York's roster of local talent was impressive. Stipe found himself reading about the likes of Blondie, Television, the Ramones and the New York Dolls, and tracing their roots back beyond the punk movement to earlier outfits like Iggy and the Stooges, the Velvet Underground and, in Britain, David Bowie and Mott the Hoople. Both Stipe and Peter Buck have since cited Patti Smith's *Horses* album as a major inspiration during their adolescent years. "That's pretty strong stuff for a 15-year-old American middle-class white boy sitting in his parents' living room with his headphones on so they wouldn't hear," Stipe once commented.

During the last two years in Illinois his personality became much more outgoing. As Collinsville's leading authority on punk rock, he had fronted his own punk band Bad Habits, took to dressing in drag at the local nightspots and was involved in a car crash that resulted in the distinctive facial scars he still bears today!

In 1978 the family moved to Watkinsville, a small town just outside of Athens, and Michael enrolled as

Peter Buck

an art student at the University of Georgia. Athens was a relatively quiet town with a population of 60,000, many of whom attended the local university. In the Sixties, that local seat of learning had earned a reputation as a thriving scene for musicians, poets and artists, consistently attracting the kind of bohemian student crowd guaranteed to respond to the excitement and novelty of punk.

The move back to Georgia found Stipe once again becoming more introverted and he claims to have spent his first six months avoiding the local nightlife and, in his own words: "maturing about five years." He still indulged his passion for punk rock by contributing to a local fanzine *Hot Java*, and even started his own magazine, *Momo*. But the first real steps towards becoming a part of the world he was reading and writing about were only taken when he went into the Wuxtry record store on East Clayton street with his closest friends, his sisters Lynda and Cyndy. There he met store assistant—and future R.E.M. guitarist—Peter Buck.

Velvet Underground—art rock supremos

Peter Buck—on the road

Peter Lawrence Buck was just over three years older than Stipe, having been born on December 6, 1956 in Oakland, California. His clan moved to San Francisco when Peter was five, before setting off again in 1966 and spending two years in Indiana. In 1970 they arrived in Roswell, a small town just outside Atlanta, Georgia. An ardent pop music fan, Buck's infatuation started with the Beatles and the Monkees and extended to the likes of the Kinks, the Rolling Stones and English glam icons such as Sweet and T-Rex. His love of music started early, too. "I started getting obsessed with rock'n'roll when I was about 12," he told the British music weekly, *New Musical Express* (*NME*).

Peter Buck—"I never wanted to be in a band."

Just as the art-rock scene in New York had influenced Stipe, it also channelled Peter's tastes away from the mainstream and towards the off-beat. Having already discovered the first Velvet Underground album, Buck's live initiation came at the age of 16 when he saw the New York Dolls in concert at Atlanta's Municipal Auditorium. Like Stipe, his knowledge of, and enthusiasm for, such underground acts as Iggy and the Stooges marked him out as different from most of his high school peers. Similarly, he too was busy raiding the local record stores and devouring copies of the *Village Voice* and *Creem* to find out more about these bands. Inspired by the music he was listening to, Buck bought his first guitar for the princely sum of $13 (about £4 at that time) and learned what he could from his brother Kenny, an experienced player.

When he was 19 Peter Buck left home. Details of the next three years are hazy and in early R.E.M. interviews the story changes from magazine to magazine. What is definitely correct is that he quit high school in 1975, enrolled at Emory University in Atlanta and began working at Doo Dahs—a local record store. There followed a period during which Buck variously claims to have been hitch-hiking around the US; cleaning toilets for two years,;and washing dishes in a restaurant in San Luis, California while sharing a house with a group of ageing hippies. This last story ends with a classic, if exaggerated, punk anecdote in which Buck blasts his house mates with the first Sex Pistols single 'Anarchy In The UK'! The chances are that all three stories have some degree of truth in them, but whatever else he got up to, Buck is known to have continued at Emory University until 1978.

"It's funny, 'cos I started getting obsessed with rock'n'roll when I was about 12. I'd read reviews and go buy records."
Peter Buck

By this time the punk scene had reached Atlanta, and local bands like the Fans and the Nasty Bucks (no relation to Peter!) kept the town's spiky-haired crowd entertained until the Sex Pistols made their Georgia debut at the Great Southeast Music Hall on January 5, 1978. Buck later claimed that he attended the gig but was thrown out by bouncers when they discovered that he didn't have a ticket. And that wasn't his only clash with authority. Having gained a reputation for occasional scrapes with the law —"just teenage stuff, nothing serious"—Peter eventually followed his brother Kenny to Athens and landed a job at a local Wuxtry's record store. His first meeting with Michael Stipe and his sisters was clearly a profound moment: "I thought, 'God! this guy's got two great-looking girlfriends. He must be pretty hip.'"

Being in a band is all right

A friendship developed when Stipe and Buck discovered a common enthusiasm for punk rock and a desire to form a band of their own. "I worked in a record store and all the musicians I met were assholes, so I never wanted to be in a band," Buck told Sandy Robertson of now-defunct British music paper *Sounds*, "Michael convinced me that it was all right!"

Stipe enjoyed a brief spell with a covers band called Gangster before starting to write songs with Buck. The success of another Georgia band, the B-52s (deranged, Fifties-style popsters most famous for their 1978 hit single 'Rock Lobster' and more recently 'Love Shack'), had inspired countless Athens-based groups who were willing to explore music beyond the area's standard southern boogie and country and western styles. Early R.E.M. contemporaries such as Pylon, the Tone-Tones and the Method Actors were formed around the university campus, playing gigs in students' apartments until the proprietors of the local nightclub—Tyrone's—realized there was money to be made out of the growing scene.

> **"Michael said he liked my eyebrows. He claims to this day that was the reason he wanted us to get together."**
> ***Bill Berry***

In the autumn of 1979 Buck moved into a shared house in Oconee Street. The building was a semi-converted church with a huge, unused space behind the main bedroom—which was quickly cleaned out and turned into a rehearsal room for local musicians. Within months Stipe had also moved in. And the house on Oconee Street quickly became a convenient crash pad for most of Athens' alternative community from regular drunken students to local dope dealers.

"It was a dumpy little shithole where only college kids could be convinced to live." complained Buck later. One of those kids was Kathleen O'Brien, a student at the university who also deejayed for the college radio, WUOG, and played in a band named after the station, Wuoggers. Her contribution to the formation of R.E.M. came when she introduced Buck and Stipe to two of Athens' latest arrivals, Bill Berry and Mike Mills.

Berry and Mills—chalk and cheese

William Thomas Berry hailed from Minnesota originally—he was born in Duluth on July 31, 1958—but by the time he started high school his family had settled in Macon, Georgia. Encouraged by his parents to take up a musical instrument, Berry chose the drums. He eventually joined the school band, whose somewhat bizarre speciality was playing Led Zeppelin's 'Whole Lotta Love' as a marching anthem for the school's football team! Berry's character combined an extrovert personality with wayward tendencies, a stark contrast to Mike Mills—his partner in the school band—who played the sousaphone (an instrument like a tuba but even larger).

Like Buck, Michael Edward Mills was born a Californian—in Orange County on December 17, 1958— but the family had soon moved to his father's home state of Georgia and settled in Macon. Mike's father was a church singer, and his mother sang and played guitar. A bright, enthusiastic pupil, Mike's short hair, glasses and quiet disposition made him an immediate target for Bill Berry.

"When we were about 14 or 15 we hated each other," admitted Berry. "He was everything I despised; great student, got along with the teachers, didn't smoke cigarettes or pot..." A truce was finally called when Berry's part-time band needed a bass player. Mills had switched from playing sousaphone to electric bass guitar and so turned up at the session. An unlikely partnership blossomed asMills and Berry saw out the rest of their school years playing covers in a number of bar bands. But by the time they graduated from high school in 1976, both were bored with the restraints of the local music scene, realizing that the Atlanta clubs were reluctant to play host to anything other than covers bands trotting out chart hits or a staple diet of the southern rock typified by Lynyrd Skynyrd and the Allman Brothers.

The two rented an apartment together in Macon. Mills went to work in the locals Sears Roebuck department store and Berry landed a

Bill Berry

B 52s—Athens' first rock stars

job as messenger at the Paragon booking agency. It was here that Berry met Miles and Ian Copeland (brothers of ex-Curved Air drummer Stewart Copeland who was soon to find fame with the Police). Ian Copeland's task was to broaden Paragon's roster of bands; which in 1977 meant introducing the company to punk rock. He found kindred spirits in Billy Berry and Mike Mills and the three formed a part time band called the Frustrations, spending their time attempting to convert Paragon's reluctant staff to the joys of the Dammed, the Sex Pistols and especially the Police.

Raising a few eyebrows

Eventually Berry and Mills decided to postpone the trauma of finding full-time employment by enrolling at the University of Georgia. Settling in Athens in January 1979, Berry joined the Wuoggers and through Kathleen O'Brien was introduced to Michael Stipe and Peter Buck. "Michael said he liked my eyebrows," Berry revealed to US magazine *Rolling Stone* in 1985.

Stipe and Buck weren't so easily convinced about Mike Mills initially, since they had first met him when he was extremely drunk in one of the local bars. Despite their doubts, the four began jamming together at the church in Oconee Street. Berry soon quit his law studies and moved into the house, where Mills was to take up almost permanent residency on the couch or any available floor space. The band plugged away diligently at covers of the Sex Pistols' 'God Save The Queen' and the Monkees' '(I'm Not Your) Stepping Stone', while also taking their first, hesitant steps at songwriting.

April 5, 1979. Kathleen O'Brien's birthday and a celebration party planned at the church. Two other local bands—Side Effects and Turtle Bay—were drafted in, but the fledgling R.E.M. (working under the name Twisted Kites) were the stars of the night's celebrations. Alongside 'God Save The Queen', the Rolling Stones' 'Honky Tonk Woman' and the Modern Lovers' 'Roadrunner', the band thundered through 15 of their own compositions. Most of these clearly showed the influences that had shaped their music, right the way through from Sixties pop to Seventies punk.

All concerned now only have hazy memories of that debut show, Peter Buck recalls the group playing for two hours with everyone in attendance being drunk. But one man sober enough to appreciate what

Bill Berry—an extrovert personality

he had seen was a local promoter who helped run the Tyrone's club—Mike Hobbs. All three of the bands that had played at the party were invited to perform at the club a week later and as the headliners were unhappy with calling themselves Twisted Kites, visitors to the church were asked to suggest a name. Suggestions varied from the helpful to the hopeless, including Negro Eyes, Slut Bank, Cans Of Piss... and R.E.M. This is an acronym which stands for Rapid Eye Movement—the condition of enhanced dreaming during a deep sleep. They played their first two proper gigs at Tyrone's, supporting local band the Brains. They also appeared at another popular Athens nightspot, the Koffee Klub.

"When I was about 13 I had just started to be a bad teenager, drinking beer and smoking pot. One of my best friends had an older brother who was just insane. He was crazy. So we'd go over to his house and smoke pot and listen to records."
Peter Buck

Triumph at the Tyrone

Attendances at both shows were so encouraging that Hobbs agreed to let the band top the bill at Tyrone's. Playing to a record crowd of 350, R.E.M.'s first headline date was on May 15, 1980, and was a huge success. "We'd been together a month and a half and we were the biggest band in town," commented Peter Buck.

Before the summer was over R.E.M had established themselves as Athens' star attraction. Although they ventured out to clubs further afield, such as the Warehouse in Atlanta, the chance to play outside Georgia didn't arise until July 1980 when they filled in for local band Pylon who had postponed three shows in North Carolina. The gigs were booked by a local record store manager, Jefferson Holt, who was so impressed by what he saw that he was to become the band's manager before the year was over.

R.E.M.'s appeal was easy to understand. American music was still largely dominated by standard adult orientated rock (AOR) in the shape of Journey, Boston, Foreigner and the British new wave of groups who had established something of a foothold with American audiences. R.E.M., however, offered a homegrown alternative to the mainstream. Combining Buck's ragged guitar dynamics with Stipe's tremulous vocals and eye catching visuals, R.E.M just demanded to be seen and heard. As his confidence grew, Stipe's performance became increasingly uninhibited and exciting to watch. One local critic branded him a "most pretentious Mick Jagger rip-off". But most of those who caught the band during their first tour of the local club circuit were entranced.

The band's songwriting was also taking on a more confident edge. Rarely venturing away from simplistic pop rock (due in no small part to their admittedly limited musical abilities), they had already developed a sound hinging largely on Buck's distinct guitar style. Buck was no virtuoso, but he didn't allow himself to be daunted by technical limitations and evolved his own style from a combination of jangling Byrds-like riffs and hooklines—a sound which would eventually become a trademark for

Mike Mills

Mike Mills—stage struck

the band. Embryonic R.E.M were captured at Tyrone's on October 4, 1980, on the bootleg *Bodycount At Tyrone's*, tearing through now long-forgotten songwriting moments like 'Smalltown Girl', 'All The Right Friends' and 'Jacques Cousteau Show'. None of these early efforts were to appear on future albums

Later that year, the 400 Watt Club opened on College Avenue, Athens, and R.E.M. found themselves with a new stamping ground. A new venue gave birth to new bands and Athens' musical community became increasingly incestuous, drummer Bill Berry moonlighting for another new band, Love Tractor. Within weeks the town's entire musical community was located in the area around Barber Street where R.E.M., the Method Actors, Pylon and the Side Effects were all living.

R.E.M. plus I.R.S. and F.B.I.

Outside the Athens scene, the story was different. R.E.M. were still struggling to find gigs with which to gain further recognition and decided to draw on the contacts made by Bill Berry and Mike Mills at the now defunct Paragon agency. Miles Copeland had just started his own label, I.R.S. Records and Ian Copeland had set up the F.B.I. booking agency—joke references from the Copeland brothers: I.R.S. to the American

Inland Revenue Service and F.B.I. the Federal Bureau of Investigation. Both were so impressed by the live R.E.M. tape Berry sent that they invited the band to support the Police at the Fox Theater, Atlanta, in December 1980. Meanwhile, record store owner Jefferson Holt had moved to Athens to open a new shop. He became the group's roadie, before taking over the booking of gigs and eventually managing the group in his spare time. His first assignment was to encourage R.E.M. to record a proper demo tape.

Under the guidance of Holt and fledgling-producer Mitch Easter (formerly of US band the Sneakers) R.E.M recorded three new compositions: 'Radio Free Europe', 'Sitting Still' and 'White Tornado' at the producer's Drive-in Studio, in April 1981. Clearly uneasy about performing in a studio, Stipe's introverted side suddenly took over and he insisted on singing while facing the furthest corner of the studio! Luckily the end result was unaffected by Stipe's sudden loss of confidence and the demo was later to be heard by some important folk in the industry.

Mitch Easter was particularly impressed, later recalling that "R.E.M. struck me as a real classic singles band." The demo tape was dispatched to record companies and magazine offices (complete with an insert card reading Do Not Open). Suitably enthralled by what he was hearing, Ian Copeland stepped in again and R.E.M. found themselves opening for English avant-garde punks the Gang of Four at the Ritz, New York.

"I worked in a music store, and all the musicians I met were assholes, so I never wanted to be in a band. Michael convinced me it was all right."
Peter Buck

The tape also came to the attention of Jonny Hibbert, a 27-year-old law student and part-time musician who was looking for a band with which to launch his own label, Hib-Tone Records. Hibbert offered them the chance to put out 'Radio Free Europe' and 'Sitting Still' as a single, on the understanding that they gave him the publishing rights (an arrangement which the band were to buy themselves out of some time later). R.E.M. returned to Drive-In Studios, "confident enough to be quietly arrogant about our talents," according to Peter Buck, and 'Radio Free Europe' was recorded again and mixed twice before Hibbert settled on the one he wanted and released it as a single. Powered by Bill Berry's clipped, decidedly new wave-style drumming, a simple, yet brilliantly effective guitar sound and a chorus that drilled its way into a listener's consciousness on first hearing, 'Radio Free Europe' was a classic slice of Eighties pop. Once a thousand copies had been given away to journalists, club owners and radio disc jockeys, R.E.M. found themselves booked into gigs as far apart as Texas, Washington D.C. and New York. Things were beginning to happen and while Hibbert hung on to his latest recruits, R.E.M. themselves were clearly looking for a bigger name as backing.

"I was determined to get other people to listen to this stuff [punk] and see what I saw in it. In this whole town there was one person who started to like this music... Bill Berry."
Ian Copeland, promoter

On the way to Chronic Town

Back at Drive-In Studios, the band set about making a follow up EP with Mitch Easter, recording six new songs: '1,000,000', 'Ages Of You', 'Gardening At Night' (which featured the earliest example of a wilfully obscure Stipe lyric), 'Carnival Of Sorts (Boxcars)', 'Stumble' and 'Jazz Lips'. Stipe claimed later that he had spent the entire recording session with a trash can over his head to get the required sound to his vocals. Elsewhere, there were various off-beat effects thrown into the mix, including an electric sitar, backwards tape loops, animal impressions and a drunken noise collage (which made up the unreleased 'Jazz Lips'). The collective musical sound crashed through diverse influences and invited comparisons with a wide range of seminal bands from the Byrds through Springsteen to the likes of Led Zeppelin—all delivered with the nervous edge of the current crop of new wave and post-punk bands..

Following a less than auspicious performance at the Beat Exchange, New Orleans, in May 1982, the band finally signed to Miles Copeland's I.R.S. label. A revised five track version of the EP was released

R.E.M.—"The biggest band in town."

in August under the title *Chronic Town*, and featured a new song 'Wolves, Lower' sitting alongside 'Gardening At Night', 'Carnival...', '1,000,000' and 'Stumble'.

Chronic Town was one of the year's most off beat and intriguing releases. The cover showed a grainy close-up of a church gargoyle, the song titles and lyrics defied the easy categorisation of so much American rock and somewhere in the track were Stipe's blurred vocals and haunting melodies. "As we went along we realized that we didn't want to be a straight narrative band that has stories in our songs," explained Buck. Bill Berry added his own mysterious comment on the release: "A 'chronic town' is a city in the state of mind."

R.E.M. were finally on their way.

FEELING GRAVITY'S PULL

If the tales Peter Buck told about adventures after leaving high school had sounded too close to the exploits of beat writer Jack Kerouac in *On The Road*, to be true, then the months following the release of *Chronic Town* gave him sufficient opportunity to experience all "that Kerouac stuff" first-hand.

I.R.S. were impressed by the band's debut recording, but the only way for R.E.M. to make themselves known was to tour. So in 1982–83 they embarked on a nomadic lifestyle; gigging night after night and only returning to Athens for a short spell before heading back out on the road. It proved to be a challenging—occasionally demoralizing—but vital experience for the group. A time which Peter Buck looks back on with equal measures of humour and disdain:

"In the old days if I was gone for a year I ate nothing but cheese sandwiches or the deli tray and slept on the floor of someone's house or in the van or in a shared room, or even worse, a bed with Mike Mills. The one time you were alone was in the shower, and maybe not then: there'd be someone shaving. The lack of privacy was mind-boggling."

The band found that their extensive touring wasn't welcomed with open arms at first. America's musical

Michael Stipe—live in London, 1982

Peter Buck—on the road

climate had changed since Peter Buck first started picking out the chords to 'God Save The Queen' in the Oconee Street rehearsal room. The country was now in the grip of a so-called British Invasion, with English artists who bridged the gap between pop and the post-punk new wave dominating the US airwaves and charts. And with the homegrown bias against bands from the South to deal with, R.E.M. found themselves facing an uphill struggle. Southern rock bands were simply perceived as being collectively hick and redneck.

Mixed receptions

Their diverse tour itinerary had them opening for a band known in America as the English Beat (in Britain just called the Beat) one night and playing to a handful of disinterested local farmers the next. The only respite from the depressing grind of half-empty bars and apathetic crowds was the prospect of a gig at one of the new wave clubs which had begun opening in many towns.

"We played an airforce base in Wichita Falls, Texas, and we were getting death threats," Peter Buck told *Sounds* when recalling those early shows.

R.E.M. supporting The Police in 1983

"There were all these crew-cut rednecks screaming for some rock'n'roll. So we played a Stones tunes. They got madder and madder. So finally I asked them what they meant by rock'n'roll and they yelled out 'Scorpions, Van Halen...'"

Meanwhile, *Chronic Town* was receiving encouraging reviews from the more enlightened sections of the music press. the *Village Voice* voted it the second best EP of 1982, while *Rolling Stone* ran a story on the band written by their former college mate Andy Slater. Keen to capitalize on their growing popularity, R.E.M. booked in at Reflection Studios in Charlotte with Mitch Easter and co-producer Don Dixon to record their debut album.

"American bands don't get signed. American bands don't get promoted. American bands don't get played on the radio."
Peter Buck

A song called 'Pilgrimage' was recorded and sent to I.R.S. for their approval. The record company had expressed misgivings about Mitch Easter's experience in a bigger studio, but they were sufficiently pleased with this first result to let him produce the forthcoming album. Considering their lack of experience in the studio, the recording process was a relatively painless one. With most of the material already written and, in some cases, already part of the band's live repertoire, it was simply a case of deciding which songs would make it onto

TV stars on The Tube

the finished record and which arrangements would be most suitable.

Intrigued by the recording opportunities that Reflection Studios offered, the band continued to experiment with various technical effects and embellishments; a cello was added on 'Talk About The Passion', the sound of Bill Berry playing pool in the room below the studio was sampled and used on 'We Walk', while backwards-guitars and an out-of-tune piano were added to 'Perfect Circle'. Expanding on singing techniques they had perfected on the road, the band also set about creating some distinctive vocal harmonies, relying heavily on Mike Mills' voice to underpin Stipe's quavering vocal. "It didn't sound like our other records, it didn't sound like us live, and it didn't sound like anything else that was coming out," insisted Peter Buck.

Murmur of satisfaction

Completed in just 25 days, *Murmur* was released in April 1983 and presented 12 songs: 'Radio Free Europe', 'Pilgrimage', 'Laughing', 'Talk About The Passion', 'Moral Kiosk', 'Perfect Circle', 'Catapult', 'Sitting Still', '9–9', 'Shaking Through', 'We Walk' and 'West Of The Fields'. There were also some songs that didn't make it onto the finished article, among them band originals 'That Beat', 'Pretty Persuasion', and 'All The Right Friends' and covers of the Velvet Underground's 'There She Goes Again' and Archie Bell and the Drells' 'Tighten Up'.

'Radio Free Europe' was once more released as a single by I.R.S. and reached Number 78 in the US singles chart. With its clipped rhythms and driving chorus, it seemed to make for a perfect introduction to R.E.M's music, although a listen to the whole album nearly 10 years on changes that impression slightly—it is the lighter side of the band that gives the greatest indication of their songwriting capabilities. Relying largely on acoustic guitars and with a seam of brittle pop melodies at their disposal, 'Perfect Circle' and 'Talk About The Passion' evoke shades of jangly, late-Sixties psychedelia and folkier influences.

"We get compared to the Byrds every day. I knew the Jam had Rickenbackers before I knew the Byrds had Rickenbackers. We've been compared to everyone from Jethro Tull to the Psychedelic Furs."
Peter Buck

"The champions of soft-focus energetic pop," wrote Richard Grabel in *NME*, before citing the Byrds and the Hollies as a convenient reference point. Peter Buck had heard that one before:

"We get compared to the Byrds every day," he agreed. *Sounds'* Bill Black claimed to hear "stern yet stirring undercurrents present in the works of Dylan and Springsteen," and commented on "the cute

R.E.M.—day of reckoning

interplay of classically American pop guitars," while offering suggestions as to what R.E.M. actually stood for: "Raw Emotional Music, Rough Energetic Music..." The response from the American media was just as encouraging—"Intelligent, enigmatic, deeply involving," gushed *Rolling Stone*.

Even at this early stage, it was Michael Stipe's lyrics that drew the most comment and seemed destined to provoke frustration and bewilderment among those raised on a more traditional style of

R.E.M.—an early photo shoot

songwriting. The general theorizing on his lyrics' significance were supplemented by insights from the band into what had inspired a particular song—amusing in the way they differed from one member to another. Stipe revealed in subsequent interviews that 'Perfect Circle' was about an old girlfriend, while Peter Buck claimed that it had been inspired by a game of touch football he had watched one night from the back porch of his house after weeks of endless touring. Apparently, the guitarist had been so exhausted and emotionally frail from time spent on the road that he'd burst into tears. He later told Stipe to capture that feeling in the song!

America for the Americans

Now at last, that quirky air that R.E.M. projected finally began to take hold back home in the US. "In America right now, the current crop of UK bands all want to be rich and famous and beautiful," Peter Buck told *Sounds*' Sandy Robertson. And while America was under siege from the likes of Culture Club, Duran Duran and Soft Cell, native audiences and the record industry were finally warming to the homegrown alternative approach of bands like R.E.M.. The post-punk fall-out had given rise to more challenging outfits like Husker Dü, the Minutemen and the Dream Syndicate. And while their appeal remained dependent on albums and live gigs, R.E.M. were deemed commercially acceptable enough to receive radio airplay. Their so-called crossover appeal was already being recognized.

I.R.S. decided that greater recognition could be

"I don't think anyone liked us. I'm glad I got to play Shea Stadium, it was cool. But the other dates were just boring."
Peter Buck

gained by exposure to bigger audiences. In August 1983 R.E.M. embarked on a five-date tour as support to the Police, playing New York's Shea, and Philadelphia's JFK, stadiums. It was not a comfortable experience and despite largely positive audience reactions, the band still insist that the tour was a mistake—"the most wretched, miserable experience of our lives," they protested.

London calling

Realizing that *Murmur* had received good reviews in the UK press, I.R.S.' next move was to plan a direct hit on British audiences. The band lined up an appearance on the popular weekly TV show *The Tube*, while dates at London's Dingwalls and the prestigious Marquee Club were also scheduled.

Their performance on *The Tube*, playing 'Talk About The Passion' (their second UK single), 'So. Central Rain' (a new song) and 'Radio Free Europe', was accomplished, if not quite the revelation some had expected. The live shows, however, drew greater praise. "This is the most vital American group of today," declared *NME*. While *Sounds'* Bill Black described them as "a classic bar-room outfit," but "too frisky to be truly frightening". Either way, there was

Stipe and Buck—on tour forever!

something here quite removed from the standard crop of rock bands flogging their wares around the UK club circuit. Visually, it was Michael Stipe who still attracted the most attention. Vying for space between Peter Buck (complete with a stock of guitar hero shapes and a cocked Rickenbacker) and the cheery, bookish Mike Mills (still the complete antithesis of a rock star) Stipe cut an intriguing figure with his mop of

"I was kinda stand-offish at college. I looked down my nose at everyone. All these people were into Grateful Dead and Hot Tuna and Little Feat."
Peter Buck

unruly curls and baggy sweater. ("Dressed down to the level of a beatnik Woody Allen," reckoned the *Sounds* writer).

By the end of 1983 *Murmur*, alongside Michael Jackson's *Thriller* and the Police's *Synchronicity*, was topping writers' polls in most of the US music press.

Peter Buck plays up for the UK, 1984.

By the time the band returned to the studio to record again at Christmas, a follow-up was attracting much interest and anticipation. Mitch Easter and Don Dixon were again brought in to take care of production duties and the band set about creating an album that was closer than either *Murmur* or the *Chronic Town* EP to the sound of R.E.M. live.

Day of Reckoning

Reckoning was recorded in two short, frantic bursts either side of Christmas 1983, and was the sound of R.E.M. captured live and largely unpolished in the Reflections Studio in Athens. The 10-song album was released in April 1984: 'Harborcoat', 'Seven Chinese Brothers', 'So. Central Rain', 'Pretty Persuasion', 'Time After Time (Annelise)', 'Second Guessing', Letter Never Sent', 'Camera', '(Don't Go Back To) Rockville' and 'Little America'.

There was the customary mix of sounds and styles, plenty of Stipe's off-beat lyricizing and in 'Pretty Persuasion' one of the band's first truly classic songs. A gorgeous rock anthem with Stipe and Mills' distinct vocalizing ,it typified the up-beat, gutsy approach of R.E.M. in full flight. Mike Mills' humorous

R.E.M.—creatively fatigued?

Peter Buck—1985

'(Don't Go Back To) Rockville' was one of the band's oldest songs, dedicated to a popular female student at the University of Athens for whom the bass player had once developed an incredible crush. 'Little America' was a narrative inspired by months spent touring and the mournful 'So. Central Rain' featured an accidental vocal fade at the end of the track when Michael Stipe fell down the stairs on which he was singing, breaking the microphone on the way down!

Reckoning reached Number 27 in the US album charts, but the two single releases—'So. Central Rain' and 'Rockville'—only scraped into the US Top 100. The media reaction was again encouraging. "They manage to celebrate everything great about white American pop music in the last 20 years," read the *Melody Maker* review. While *Sounds* picked out the song 'Rockville' as possessing "four chords that will shake the world."

"The second album shows the world whether you're dealing with a worthless bunch of talentless

"I still hear '*Murmur*, best thing you've ever done'. Well, you just wiped out the Eighties and Nineties for me, thank you very much."
Peter Buck

hacks who had a lucky idea, or a good band," said Peter Buck, succinctly. "It was our day of reckoning. This had to be something that would find you or leave you cold."

Following the album's release it was decided to make a video to accompany the first side of the record. Stipe was the only member of the band who had taken an active interest in the video medium and none of them had been enamoured with the promo for 'Radio Free Europe' they had made the year before. The band felt uncomfortable with the video medium and, particularly as it had been their first effort, they hadn't even been sure of what they wanted to convey. This time around they recruited former Athens art teacher Jim Herbert and a suitably off-beat promo titled *Left Of Reckoning* was made, featuring a collage of film clips of the group running amok in local sculptor Bill Miller's whirligig garden.

Early in 1984, while taking time off between recording and touring, Buck, Berry and Mills had hooked up with an old friend, Bryan Cook, and singer/songwriter Warren Zeavon to form their own side project, the Hindu Love Gods. They gigged in the Athens area and even recorded a single, featuring live versions of 'Narrator' (an old R.E.M. song) and the Easybeats' 'Gonna Have A Good Time Tonight'.

'Green Grow The Rushes.'

Between further bouts of touring Buck also found time to play on the Replacements' *Let It Be* album. The Replacements were the kind of spirited garage pop band with which R.E.M. readily identified. Back on the road, they brought along two other like-minded bands, the Dream Syndicate and The dbs (featuring future R.E.M. 'fifth member' David Holsapple), as support, and continued to spread their own version of the punk ethos as an antidote to the bland and faceless music which they felt was still dominating America. Buck even put pen to paper and wrote an essay entitled

'The true spirit of American rock' for the US magazine *Record* in which he criticized the complacency of American audiences and the mistaken belief that the only good rock music in 1984 was British.

Peter Buck in Newcastle, 1986

Time of Reconstruction

A third album, to be called *Fables Of The Reconstruction*, was begun just months after the band had completed *Reckoning*, recorded at Livingstone Studios in North London with veteran producer Joe Boyd, whose previous credits included folk-rock band Fairport Convention and guitarist Richard Thompson. The studio had been Boyd's choice and the band were keen enough on working with him to agree to a protracted stay in London. However, compared to the *Murmur* and *Reckoning* sessions, the recording process for *Fables Of The Reconstruction* was not an easy one. A tight schedule meant that the band had less than a fortnight to write an album's worth of material, and a combination of homesickness and creative fatigue put them under immense pressure.

There were 11 songs on *Fables Of Reconstruction*, which was released in June 1985: 'Feeling Gravity's Pull', 'Maps And Legends', 'Driver 8', 'Life And How To Live It', 'Old Man Kensey', 'Can't Get There From

Here', 'Green Grow The Rushes', 'Kohoutek', 'Auctioneer (Another Engine)', 'Good Advices' and 'Wendell Gee'.

Despite sporadic bursts of genius, especially on 'Driver 8' and the quirky power pop of 'Life And How To Live It' and 'Can't Get There From Here', there was an overwhelmingly dour atmosphere which seemed to permeate each and every track and denied the record the uplifting, positive edge that had been so evident on the first two albums. Stipe assumed the role of storyteller on songs like 'Old Man Kensey' which was based on a real-life tale of a dog kidnapper, prompting Buck to describe *Fables Of The Reconstruction* as "Michael's storytelling record".

"Pop music for most people is really bland. You don't have to understand it. It's just this boring little nothing."
Peter Buck

The music press was less sympathetic: "R.E.M. don't aim for much more than enigma," grumbled the *Village Voice*. And within months, the band themselves were agreeing. Too long away from home and too long in each others company, *Fables Of The Reconstruction* sounded like the work of a band desperate to take stock of their situation and allow themselves a chance to reassess what they were doing. Claimed Peter Buck, with admirable honesty: "Every song was an expression of how depressed we were feeling."

Michael Stipe—a close shave in 1985

IT'S THE END OF THE WORLD AS WE KNOW IT (AND I FEEL FINE)

Michael Stipe—blonds have more fun.

If anything, 1985 should be remembered as the year of Michael Stipe's most dramatic changes of image. The mass of blond curls that had grown the year before were suddenly cropped, and it was a shaven-headed Stipe who tottered on stage in Glasgow, Scotland, with the word DOG scrawled across his forehead. As the gig progressed, the heat from the stage lights caused him to sweat and this covered his face in smudged rivers of black ink. When quizzed about the incident in the music press, the singer complained that bad British food and a stomach infection had left him feeling like a dog! At later shows he bleached his newly grown hair peroxide blond—sometimes dyeing it with mustard—and covered his eyelids in black mascara; his appearance often altering from one show to the next.

Throughout the 1985 tour private in-jokes,

unusual mascots and props came into play as a means of alleviating the boredom and frustration of long spells on the road. All four members of the band took to taking bicycles with them on tour. Stipe, who had always been a keen cyclist, suggested using the bicycle as a band symbol. Never ones to fight shy of imagery, and with a growing cult following that seemed to hang on every one of Stipe's bizarre utterances, R.E.M. began to display the bicycle image on tickets and handbills for the tour promoting *Fables Of The Reconstruction* and in the background of new band photos. It was perhaps inevitable that Stipe's bicycle even turned up on stage one night.

Bicycle touring

Unfortunately, road stress led to various incidents on-stage and off. One interviewer found Peter Buck hiding on the tour bus after an avid fan had offered him the use of his girlfriend for the night! And the media were quick to publicize a tantrum at an R.E.M. performance at New York's Beacon Theater. The band had scooped the New Music award from the *College Music Journal* and played a set which was taped for broadcast on MTV. Halfway through 'Can't Get There From Here', Peter Buck sent his guitar flying through the air before storming off stage.

Michael Stipe—monk rocker!

Problems with the on-stage monitors were cited as the reason for the outburst.

Elsewhere R.E.M. found themselves playing to audiences of vastly differing sizes. In some parts of

R.E.M.—a pause for thought

the US they would be packing 500-capacity clubs, while the following night's gig would find them struggling to fill smaller arenas. In certain areas their popularity was extraordinary, in others they were still largely unknown. Meanwhile, their cult following in Britain remained fanatical but was clearly not enough for them to achieve any major breakthrough. Singles were released and the band booked in for another UK tour (including two sold-out shows at London's Hammersmith Palais) but recognition from UK radio was almost nonexistent.

It was this obscurity which frustrated I.R.S.. Faced with the prospect of making another album, R.E.M. reiterated their intention not to compromise

"I think in many ways we're much more down to earth than many rock bands, because we don't go in for that rock'n' roll myth."
Mike Mills

or force themselves in a more overtly commercial direction just to increase sales or score a hit single. I.R.S. were willing to accept this no-compromise approach, but were still left bemused by their wayward charges' reluctance to support bigger bands and follow the established path to greater recognition. In hindsight, it was the shrewd business acumen of manager Jefferson Holt and their attorney Bertis Downs that helped R.E.M. maintain their no-compromise position. Holt had been a part of the R.E.M. camp since 1980, and just as the band had risen in stature since their days on the Athens club circuit, so had his experience and reputation. Supported by a solid team R.E.M. set about planning their next move.

This turned out to be getting back to work. American producer Don Gehman had been less than enthralled by *Fables Of The Reconstruction* but was sufficiently intrigued by what he had heard to consider working with R.E.M.. Gehman had recently worked with US singer/songwriter John Cougar Mellencamp, whose work had impressed the band. He flew to Athens to meet the group and explained his intention to focus their sound and guide them away from the the listlessness that had

R.E.M.—almost breaking through

HAMPTON

"It's funny, because for years we would make a record and go on tour and do like three or four new songs. And every time, the next year's hit single was one of the new songs. The next year they're screaming for that one they didn't notice the time before."

Peter Buck

dominated the last record. I.R.S. approved the collaboration and the band decamped to Bloomington, Indiana, to start work on album number four.

Joining the Pageant

Bloomington was an ideal place for R.E.M. to work. As a college town it was comparable to Athens, while the lakeside apartments in which the band were

Bill Berry—'Driver 8'

> **"Our intuition has been more valuable to us than any of the great words of wisdom passed on to us by the damned record company."**
> ***Bill Berry***

housed and Gehman's insistence that the band didn't work for longer than eight hours a day made for a more relaxed and productive atmosphere. In keeping with the spirit of fun, it was decided that the new album's title would be *Life's Rich Pageant*, a catchphrase of spoof detective Inspector Clouseau in the Peter Sellers comedy movie *A Shot In The Dark*.

Life's Rich Pageant was released in July 1986 and, one better than *Fables Of The Reconstruction*, was a 12-song compilation: 'Begin The Begin', 'These Days', 'Fall On Me', 'Cuyahoga', 'Hyena', 'Underneath The Bunker', 'The Flowers Of Guatemala', 'I Believe', 'What If We Give It Away?', 'Just A Touch', 'Swan Swan H' and 'Superman'.

Peter Buck—on-stage in Houston 1986

R.E.M. in Texas, 1986

'Fall On Me' was the first song to be recorded and was a tuneful exercise in pure pop, today still considered by many to be among the best songs R.E.M. have ever written. 'I Believe' contained furious banjo picking, a rush of acoustic guitar and a soaring chorus. And revamped old song, 'Just A Touch', seemed to be a definite throwback to the band's punk roots. Another direction was taken with 'What If We Give It Away', a reworking of an old R.E.M. live favourite previously titled 'Get On Their Way', while 'Hyena' was left over from the *Fables Of The Reconstruction* sessions. Continuing their penchant for obscure cover versions as B-sides and out-takes, a version of the Clique's 'Superman' became the first cover to actually make it onto an R.E.M. album.

Stipe's lyrics continued to follow a path all their own—much to Don Gehman's occasional chagrin—but also started to touch on politics and world affairs. Despite the obscure word-play and abstract images, it's clear Stipe used the album to voice opinions on Washington's involvement in Central America ('The Flowers Of Guatemala'), the threat of nuclear war ('Hyena'), the growing problem of acid rain ('Fall On Me') and the injustice suffered by American Indians ('Cuyahoga').

Michael Stipe—making movies

Life's Rich Pageant peaked at Number 21 in the US album charts, andthe first single 'Fall On Me' reached the Top 5 in many of the country's rock radio playlists without actually becoming a national hit. Nevertheless, by January 1987 the album had been certified gold—without a hit single to promote it, R.E.M. had still managed to sell 500,000 copies. Reflecting on the album a year later Peter Buck was justifiably pleased: "I think we made the perfect record that we could in that style". With its emphasis on lush arrangements and a powerful delivery, *Life's Rich Pageant* seemed to capture R.E.M. from a different angle.

Outside interests

Away from the group, all four members continued to pursue outside activities, throwing themselves into side projects and one-offs. Earlier that year, Athens had been the subject of a full-length documentary. *Athens, Ga—Inside/Out* was directed by their former colleague and local art teacher Jim Herbert. Michael

Michael Stipe—portrait of the artist as a young man

Stipe's involvement was noticeable by the amount of coverage his favourite local bands received and by the inclusion of two R.E.M. songs on the film's soundtrack: a cover of the Everly Brothers' '(All I Have To Do Is) Dream' and a band original 'Swan Swan H.'. He kept himself busy later that year as well, recording with the Golden Palominos and producing local musician Hugh Largo.

The other members of the band weren't idle either. Buck, Berry and Mills regrouped with Warren Zeavon to play on his *Sentimental Hygiene* album. Mike Mills produced an album for the band Waxing Poetics and Peter Buck produced the Feelies' *The Good Earth* album and Dream So Real's *Father's House* . At one point Peter even ended up back at Wuxtry's Record Store working behind the counter getting paid in free albums—until continuous plagues of autograph hunters forced him to quit the job. Bill Berry, however, escaped from the recording studio and married his long-time girlfriend Mary.

"I guess I really focus to detail more than the grand picture, and that detail becomes the words to the song. And given the detail, I guess it's left up to the listener to spot it and put a frame around it."
Michael Stipe

Dead Letter day

The following year I.R.S. capitalized on the success of *Life's Rich Pageant* by releasing a compilation of R.E.M. B-sides and rareties. Peter Buck supervised the collection, sifting through seven years' worth of tapes to find the right material. "Listening to this album should be like browsing through a junk shop," he explained, jokingly.

Released in April 1987, *Dead Letter Office* contained a mammoth 15 songs: 'Crazy' (an old Pylon number and the B-side of the 'Driver-8' single), 'There She Goes Again' (a Velvet Underground cover and the B-side of the I.R.S. release of 'Radio Free Europe'), 'Burning Down' (B-side of the UK double pack single 'Wendell Gee'), 'Voice Of Harold' (B-side of the UK 12-inch single 'So. Central Rain'), 'Burning

***R.E.M.—part of* Life's Rich Pageant**

Michael Stipe says it with flowers.

Hell' (B-side of the UK 12-inch version of 'Can't Get There From Here'), 'White Tornado' (B-side of the single 'Superman'), 'Toys In The Attic' (an Aerosmith cover and the B-side of the UK 12-inch single 'Fall On Me'), 'Windout' (from the *Bachelor Party* soundtrack), 'Ages Of You' (extra track on the B-side of the UK double pack single 'Wendell Gee'), 'Pale Blue Eyes' (a Lou Reed cover), 'Rotary Ten' (B-side of the 'Fall On Me' single), 'Bandwagon' (B-side of the 'Can't Get There From Here' single), 'Femme Fatale' (B-side of the UK 12-inch single 'Superman), 'Walter's Theme' (an out-take from *Reckoning*) and 'King Of The Road' (a Roger Miller cover and B-side of 'So. Central Rain').

Buck's sleeve notes gave a brief background to each number, while freely admitting that some of the material was less than spectacular (the jokey 'Walter's Theme' and the heavy-metal pastiche of 'Burning Hell' being singled out in particular). The album's release was accompanied by *R.E.M. Succumbs*—a collection of their promo videos to date ('Radio Free Europe', 'So. Central Rain, 'Can't Get There From Here', 'Driver 8' and 'Fall On Me'), a segment of Jim Herbert's film *Left Of Reckoning* and live footage to accompany 'Feeling Gravity's Pull' and

Waiting for the show

"The whole album is about chaos. I've become very interested in chaos."
Michael Stipe on
Document

‘Life And How To Live It’. There was some irony in the video’s title and in its actual release. It seemed to be an acknowledgement that Stipe was still the only member of R.E.M. who was enthusiastic about the video medium, while Peter Buck had told *Creem* magazine that “I’ve never seen a video that made me like a song. Ours, I think, are half-dumb and half-intelligent. I give so little thought to it that I don’t really care.”

It was Don Gehman who suggested R.E.M. use New York-born producer Scott Litt to produce a new song ‘Romance’, which the band were recording for a forthcoming film soundtrack. R.E.M. had just completed the 1986 tour and while the result of their first collaboration with Litt was less than brilliant, a rapport was still quickly struck up. The band believed that Gehman had been less than satisfied with *Life’s Rich Pageant*. He had expressed doubts over whether they would ever have a hit single, but has since claimed in interviews that he would have liked to have worked with the band again. However, it was Scott Litt who sat behind the production desk of the Nashville Sound Emporium when the band began work on their fifth album.

Peter Buck—waiting for the bubble to burst

Commenting on their decision to work with Litt, Peter Buck explained why the band didn't consider Don Gehman suitable for the project: "The new songs, because of the way we wrote them, wouldn't have lent themselves to that big AOR thing."

The most noticeable aspect of the new material were Michael Stipe's rather more audible vocals. The muffled sound of the past had been replaced with a much greater clarity, giving the material a keener edge. Some suggested that R.E.M. were finally bowing to commercial pressure and that the overt pop melodies and crystal clear vocals were indicative of this change; something the band denied. "We didn't set out to mix the vocals louder, it just seemed natural," explained Mike Mills. "There was a point where we sat back and listened to it and realized that the vocals were clearer and more out-front, but nobody had really noticed it or worried about it up to that point."

Important Document

Titled simply *Document* (although with the words 'R.E.M. No. 5' on the sleeve and the cryptic message 'File Under Fire' on the spine), the album was released in September 1987: 'Finest

Michael Stipe and Spiderman!

"I recognize when the caricature is getting out of hand and I pull back and recognize when it needs to go further and I push it."
Michael Stipe

Worksong', 'Welcome To The Occupation', 'Exhuming McCarthy', 'Disturbance At The Heron House', 'It's The End Of The World As We Know It (And I Feel Fine)', 'The One I Love', 'Fireplace', 'Lightnin' Hopkins', 'King Of Birds' and 'Oddfellows Local 151'—10 tracks in all.

The first taster of the new R.E.M. album came with the release of 'The One I Love' as a single in the US in August. It had already been played on the 1986 tour and was a potent, dramatic rock song, with one of Stipe's bitterest lyrics. Although loosely described as a song of betrayal, the singer denied that it was autobiographical. However, lines like "This one goes out to the one I left behind" and the sheer emotion

On top of the world

R.E.M.—by the wayside

charging through the verses were hints enough to leave critics pondering exactly what had inspired this soul searching.

As a body of work *Document* was R.E.M.'s most focussed and accessible record There was the bouncing riff and energy of 'Finest Worksong', while 'Welcome To The Occupation' was a jangling throwback to the folksier R.E.M. of old, and 'Exhuming McCarthy' offered a politically charged dig

"Halfway through the tour we were so burned out by it we were just on stage going through the motions. We really felt we were robbing the audience of what they deserve."
Bill Berry

at the Reagan administration. A frantic cover of Wire's 'Strange' jostled for space with the wistful, naggingly-tuneful 'It's The End Of The World As We Know It (And I Feel Fine)', while Stipe kept his followers happy with another infuriatingly ambiguous lyric on the cryptic 'Disturbance At The Heron House'. "The whole album is about chaos," revealed the singer. "I've become very interested in chaos and the hypothesis that there is order within chaos, so I guess that kind of carried over into the recording".

Reviewers were quick to spot the themes of trouble and confusion. "More violent and more whimsical than any other R.E.M. album to date," claimed *Melody Maker*. The same paper's Allan Jones, in his interview with the band, offered the opinion that *Document* was "stripped of ornamental diversions" suggesting that, despite good reviews, some of the band's followers had considered *Life's Rich Pageant* overly produced and lacking in the raw quality that made its successor such a strong record.

The Number 1 I Love

When questioned, producer Scott Litt admitted that the band had wanted to record the kind of songs that would get played on the radio. And R.E.M. achieved their objective. Litt had bet Bill Berry that 'The One I Love' would be a hit single. He won the bet as the song scrambled into the US Top 10, peaking at Number 9 in December. Meanwhile *Document* became R.E.M.'s first US Top 20 album, and was their first million-seller by January 1988. In a brazen display of American fervour *Rolling Stone* embellished its December 1987 cover with a picture of R.E.M. and the words 'America's Best Rock'n'Roll Band'.

The next single, 'It's The End Of The World As We Know It (And I Feel Fine)', failed to match the success of 'The One I Love', as did 'Finest Worksong', but R.E.M. were now acknowledged as one of the few cult bands to have crossed over to the

"America's Best Rock'N'Roll Band."

> **"More violent and more whimsical than any other R.E.M. album to date."**
> ***Mat Smith, music critic***

mainstream. Their five-year contract with I.R.S. was coincidentally drawing to a close and the Warner Brothers label began to express an interest in 'America's Best Rock'n'Roll Band'. It was almost inevitable that the group would move on.

Though he would be deeply disappointed to this day about the band's defection, I.R.S.'s vice president Jay Boberg was forced to admit that a larger label would be able to offer the band the greater exposure they needed in other countries. I.R.S. planned another world tour to promote *Document*, but the band declined.

Finally Lenny Waronker, president at Warner Brothers, offered a deal too good to be refused: strong distribution in other territories, no pressure to compromise themselves musically (the label had already signed 'alternative' acts such as the

R.E.M.—Holland, 1992

Replacements and Husker Dü) and record advances of reputedly \$2–3 million (well over £1 million at the time). Unable to match these figures I.R.S. made a last-ditch attempt to keep the band by offering higher royalties on their back catalogue. But, believing that a larger company could offer more than just greater financial rewards, R.E.M. signed to Warner Brothers.

Cashing in on the name

Not surprisingly, I.R.S. capitalized on the recent success of the band by releasing a best-of compilation titled *Eponymous* in October 1988. The 12-strong tracklisting ran: 'Radio Free Europe', 'Gardening At Night', 'Talk About The Passion', 'So. Central Rain', '(Don't Go Back To) Rockville', 'Can't Get There From Here', 'Driver 8', 'Romance', 'Fall On Me', 'The One I Love', 'Finest Worksong' and 'It's The End Of The World As We Know It (And I Feel Fine)'. R.E.M. collectors were offered an added incentive with alternative mixes of 'Radio Free Europe', 'Gardening At Night' and 'Finest Worksong' and the inclusion of 'Romance' from the soundtrack of the 1986 movie *Made In Heaven*.

Meanwhile R.E.M. had shelved plans to take some time off, in favour of recording the follow-up to *Document*. They began work with Scott Litt at Ardent

Michael Stipe—live in London, 1989

Studios, Memphis, and found themselves faced with one of the toughest challenges of their career. As a direct reference to the band's awareness of ecological issues it was decided that the new record would be called, simply, *Green*. Their main objective was to make a record that didn't sound like '*Document II*'. The intelligent rock stance of songs like 'The One I Love' and 'Finest Worksong' had suggested to some critics that R.E.M. were now perceived as an arena rock band in the mould of U2. Their move to bigger venues and greater popularity seemed to confirm this impression. *Green* was designed to dispel those notions.

Going Green

Released in November 1988, *Green* contained: 'Pop Song '89', 'Get Up', 'You Are The Everything', 'Stand', 'World Leader Pretend', 'The Wrong Child', 'Orange Crush', 'Turn You Inside Out', 'Hairshirt', 'I Remember California' and an untitled 11th song featuring Peter Buck on drums.

The album's most distinctive track was 'Orange Crush', a strident commentary on the effects of the chemical Agent Orange in the Vietnam War (although Stipe in typically mischievous fashion is reported to have said that the song was actually about the popular soft drink). It begged comparisons with U2. The rattling guitar lines brought to mind the playing style of the Edge from U2, while whirring helicopter sound effects and dominant chorus all sounded much like the work of the Irish superstars, nudging R.E.M. ever closer to the Stadium Rock bracket they seemed so keen to avoid.

In contrast 'Pop Song '89' was a far simpler and less bombastic opening song than either of those on the previous two albums, while 'Get Up' and 'Stand' were noticeable for their almost throwaway melodies and quirky appeal. Mandolins and acoustic instrumentation dominated the gentle 'You Are The Everything' and 'Hairshirt'. R.E.M. even admitted that

R.E.M.—reluctant rock stars

they had originally wanted the whole of the album's second half to be acoustic.

In contrast to the darker mood of the *Document* album, *Green* seemed almost obsessively cheery. Lyrically, Stipe matched the naive simplicity of the music with intentionally dumb lyrics, while returning to more serious subject matter on 'Orange Crush' and 'The Wrong Child' (about a disabled youth) and the revealing 'World Leader Pretend'—in which Stipe seemed to admit that there was an element of manipulation in his role as R.E.M.'s frontman, and that the mystique was deliberate. "I know what I am doing," he confessed to the British music magazine *Q*. "I recognize when that caricature is getting out of hand and I pull back, and I recognize when it needs to go further and I push it." If it was a caricature, the critics liked it.

"*Green* whistles up an intriguing collage of American myth and personal wonder," declared *Sounds*, giving the album four out of five possible stars. But this time the American music press were less sympathetic to R.E.M.'s latest effort, suggesting that the move to a bigger record label had resulted in a weaker record.

Mike Mills—looking ahead

"I think we made the perfect record we could in that style. And the new songs, because of the way we wrote them, wouldn't have lent themselves to that big AOR thing."
Peter Buck on Document.

Peter Buck—throwing shapes

Realizing that *Green* was unlikely to live up to Warner Brothers' expectations in terms of sales, producer Scott Litt had warned the company, some months before, not to expect a five-million selling record. His prediction was right. Disappointingly, *Green* only peaked at Number 15 in the US Top 20, although as the band were quick to point out, I.R.S.'s *Eponymous* compilation had probably stolen some of their thunder. Undeterred, one of R.E.M.'s most outspoken supporters *Rolling Stone* began 1989 by putting them on their cover—again—and in another display of American fervour pronounced them 'America's Hippest Band'.

NEAR WILD HEAVEN

While R.E.M.'s success and popularity as a band was clearly growing, their private lives remained just that. All four members of the band still lived in Athens, and new students at the University of Georgia soon overcame their initial star-spotting and grew used to seeing Michael Stipe checking out one of the local bands at the nightspots R.E.M. had been playing just three years earlier.

Michael Stipe and Jim McKay (centre), editing Tourfilm

Meanwhile, the group's growing political awareness soon manifested itself in a rigorous interest in local politics. Determined to give something back to the community that had nurtured them for so long, a newly-founded company R.E.M./Athens Ltd donated $5,000 (around £2,000) to preserve historic local buildings when the city council could not raise the money. Never one to fight shy of declaring his views, the 1988 US Election campaign found Michael Stipe voicing his support for the Democratic candidate Michael Dukakis—and even taking out full-page advertisements in the local press urging fellow Athenians to vote the same way.

Some business on the side

During the lengthy mixing process of the *Green* album, all of R.E.M. had become sidetracked by outside musical projects. The band's most

Michael Stipe—putting on an act

persistent moonlighter Peter Buck hooked up with Robyn Hitchcock for his 1988 tour and *Queen Elvis* album, guested on country rock band Drivin'n'Cryin's *Mystery Road* album, financed the release of a live record by Atlanta's local punk heroes the Fans and still found time to marry his girlfriend Barrie—who was co-manageress of the latest 400 Watt Club in Mexico.

Bill Berry worked with local singer/songwriter Michelle Malone on her album *New Experience*. Mike Mills produced the album *Sixes And Sevens* for another Athens group, Billy James. And even R.E.M. manager Jefferson Holt found time to release his own album *Come On Here If You Want To* — a shambolic collection of cover versions—under the name Vibrating Egg.

Michael Stipe collaborated with the Roches and Natalie Merchant from the band 10,000 Maniacs for a cover of 'Little April Showers' on the Walt Disney

"I've never written an outright love song, and I'm not sure that of the eleven songs on this record I've written an outright love song, but I'm trying."
Michael Stipe on
Out Of Time

R.E.M.—take it to the bridge

tribute album *Stay Awake* (something which, along with the time spent with Merchant on an earlier tour, prompted strong, but unconfirmed, rumours of a romance), he produced his sister Lynda's band Hetch Hetchy for the independent label Texas Hotel and began work on his own, still unreleased solo album under the working title *Field Recordings*. With film maker Jim McKay he formed the C-00 Film Corps and set about producing music videos for various artists, including his latest discovery the Chickasaw Mudd Puppies and ex-Black Flag frontman Henry Rollins, before turning his attention to R.E.M.'s future promo videos. Their first effort was the video for 'Pop Song '89', featuring Stipe and three female friends—all bare-chested—dancing. The band's popularity was now such that MTV were forced to play it (although the nipples were censored!). This release was followed by an 85-minute live film linked to the *Green* album—*Tourfilm*.

Peter Holsapple—making five

1989 found R.E.M. working harder than ever before. To take the pressure off Peter Buck a second guitarist was added to the touring line-up of R.E.M. This was long-time friend of the band, and former guitarist with The dbs, Peter Holsapple. And when R.E.M. got back into live mode, the tour following the release of *Green* included the US, Europe, Britain, Japan and first time visits to Australia and New Zealand, where the band were particularly well-received. Despite the album's slow start, the first single 'Stand' reached Number 6 in the US charts and, combined with the rigorous touring schedule, helped boost sales of the album considerably over the coming months.

"The last two records of ours have been fairly political albums. And I wanted to move away from that, so as not to pigeonhole myself as a political writer."
Michael Stipe on **Out Of Time**

Playing such large arenas, as they were now obliged to do, did not sit easily with the band. As a way of showing just how uneasy they felt, they took to playing with a large screen on stage behind them flashing up typical 'rockspeak' messages—'Are you ready to rock'n'roll'—which were designed to poke fun at the shallow gesturing of most 'big-time' rock bands. Whether the irony was lost on some members of the audience is hard to tell. Peter Buck, in particular, was dismissive of the atmosphere at larger gigs, admitting to *Rolling Stone* that he preferred to see bands playing in smaller venues. Yet it seemed that whatever reservations the members of R.E.M. may have had about their new-found status, the rest of the world was determined to heap praise upon them. Arriving in Britain to perform their new UK single 'Orange Crush' on *Top of the Pops* and play two sold-out nights at London's Hammersmith Odeon, they found

Michael Stipe—under the sun

themselves gracing the cover of the *Sunday Observer* magazine alongside the lofty headline, 'The Best Band In The World'.

All burnt out

However, by the final leg of the tour the band were understandably exhausted, and the relative commercial failure of subsequent singles, 'Pop Song '89' and 'Get Up', in comparison with the success of 'Stand', resulted in their popularity dipping again towards the end of the trip. During the first half they had managed to sell out New York's Madison Square Gardens in just under an hour; months later they found themselves once again struggling to fill venues—which suggested that many of their earlier audience were now staying away, disgruntled by

Natalie Merchant of 10,000 Maniacs

> **"I like my life. I'm 31, I'm one-fourth of an incredibly successful pop band, I sit around, people come to me, talk to me, photograph me..."**
> ***Michael Stipe***

the band's elevation to so-called 'arena' rock status. While *Green* had come close to bringing R.E.M. into the mainstream, the task had not quite been completed. "Halfway through the tour we were so burned out by it we were just on stage going through the motions," explained Bill Berry. "We really felt we were robbing the audience of what they deserve. The whole thing was pretty depressing." It was then, as the tour finally ground to a halt, that the band vowed not to return to the live circuit for the immediate future. Besides, another album was already being planned that would prove to be R.E.M.'s most significant recording yet.

Band activity in the Nineties began with the release of *Pop Screen*—a collection of promo videos from *Document* and *Green*. Following this Stipe toured Eastern Europe with UK singer/songwriter Billy Bragg and Natalie Merchant, while Buck, Berry and Mills completed work on the Hindu Love Gods album with singer Warren Zeavon. The result of a drunken after-hours session in the recording studio, the album featured cover versions ranging from old blues to Prince's 'Raspberry Beret'. Commented Bill Berry: "It took us about as long to do as it takes to listen to."

R.E.M.—made in the shade

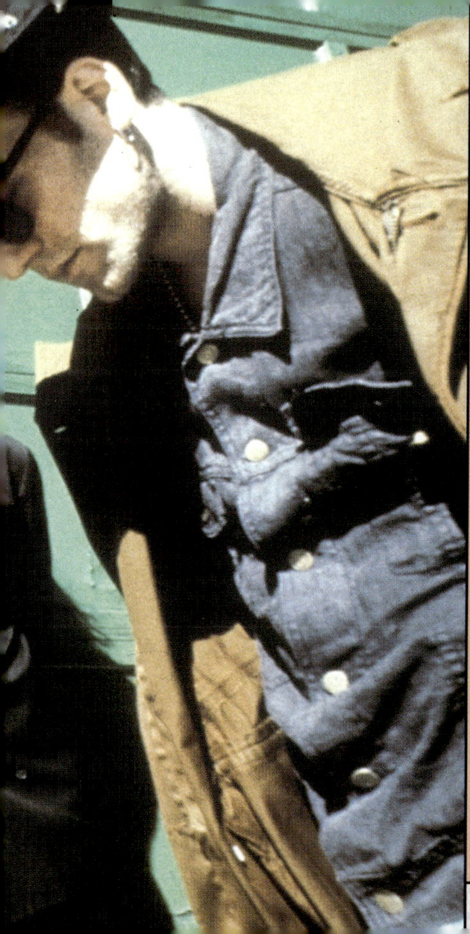

"I went to the Grammys one time, and the show itself is a stultifyingly boring piece of shit."
Peter Buck

The band had not planned to begin rehearsals for the new album until March, but by January 1990 Buck and Mills had started working on new ideas and were soon to be joined by Bill Berry. Right from the start the three of them decided to switch instruments in an attempt to distance themselves from their usual way of writing. Buck avoided his usual electric guitar and chose an acoustic mandolin, while Mills handed his bass over to Berry and switched to piano.

When Stipe joined them after six weeks, he found the rest of R.E.M.—under Buck's guidance—determined to make an album as far removed from both *Green* and *Document* as they could. With Mills writing almost exclusively on the keyboard, second guitarist Peter Holsapple was brought in to take care of extra bass and guitar duties. It soon became

Michael Stipe—pose for thought

Mike Mills and Peter Buck—jangling in unison!

apparent that this latest R.E.M. record would favour a more acoustic and less arena rock-based sound than anything they had done before. With Scott Litt taking care of production, the band began recording backing tracks at Bearsville Studios, Woodstock, in September, moving to John Keane's Athens Studio for overdubs before finally mixing at Prince's Paisley Park Studios, Minneapolis, in December.

The band's reluctance to tour enabled them to experiment with as many new sounds as they liked and, knowing that they wouldn't have to recreate the songs live on stage, they let their imagination take over. Alongside Peter Holsapple, the album featured a cast of extras: The Atlanta Symphony Orchestra, B-52's vocalist Kate Pierson, New Orleans sax player Kidd Jordan and rapper KRS-One.

Out Of Time—at the top

Out Of Time—so named by Mike Mills when Warner Brothers started pressuring the band for a title—was released in March 1991 with: 'Radio Song', 'Losing My Religion', 'Low', 'Near Wild Heaven', 'Endgame', 'Shiny Happy People', 'Belong', 'Half A World Away', 'Texarkana', 'Country Feedback' and 'Me In Honey'.

The first single 'Losing My Religion' was the perfect taster for the new album, with a lyric steeped in melancholy, a jangling refrain and the kind of chorus that was guaranteed to snag its way into the sub-conscious after one hearing. It was less overblown than 'Finest Worksong' or 'Orange Crush' and the band seemed to have struck the ideal balance between power and pomp. Described by Stipe as a "classic love song", it was one of many similar productions to be found on *Out Of*

Time.. "The last two albums of ours have been fairly political albums," he agreed, "and I wanted to move away from that, so as not to pigeonhole myself as a political writer. I'm not sure that of the 11 songs on this record I've written an outright love song, but I'm trying! The record is about love and it's about memory and it's about time. Those are three things that for me as a songwriter are pretty new territory."

Mike Mills' involvement in the album, which had included arranging the strings on most of the tracks, was immediately noticeable with his lead vocal on 'Near Wild Heaven' and 'Texarkana'. He was also part of a shared vocal, along with the B-52's Kate Pierson and Stipe, on the album's most surprising

Michael Stipe—waiting for a number one album

song 'Shiny Happy People'. Using the same musical simplicity they had employed on 'Stand' and 'Get Up' from the *Green* album, 'Shiny Happy People' was the record's most commercial and immediate moment. Almost infuriatingly good-natured, it seemed to glow with doe-eyed optimism, reflected in Stipe's grinning vocal and a nursery-rhyme guitar sound. "It's a relentless, mindless, upbeat happy song," laughed Peter Buck. Coming from equally off-beat directions were 'Radio Song', a curious merge of rock and rap, 'Endgame', a meandering instrumental with an ethereal chorus of 'la-la's' and the plodding, downbeat 'Low'.

"I'm afraid it might be too weird for some people. I'm afraid they might not get it," confessed Bill Berry, when questioned about *Out Of Time* just after its recording, but his fears proved to be groundless. The album reached the US Top 5 within three weeks of its release and by May 1991 R.E.M. had their first American Number 1 album.

Alternative solutions

While it can hardly be denied that *Out Of Time* was one of the best, if not *the* best, albums R.E.M. had made, there were other factors at work which contributed to the band's long overdue acceptance. After years of steady bombardment from such 'underground' artists as the Replacements, Husker Du and, of course, R.E.M., the American mainstream had finally begun to embrace the so-called alternative musical culture. R.E.M. hardly fitted in with any convenient musical genre, alternative or otherwise,

"It's out of time, out of place. It's not really fitting in with what's going on in music right now."
Michael Stipe on
Out Of Time

but that wasn't surprising—their curious blend of Sixties pop, folk, a style of rock with obvious punk roots and a distinct non-image had always been the antithesis of everything else around them. Now their time had come. American rock—for so long the domain of big hair, spandex and empty posturing—was finally showing signs of positive change. An 'alternative' rock sound, courtesy of acts like Faith No More, Living Colour and the Red Hot Chili Peppers, had started to jam the airwaves, fill clubs and sell records in surprisingly large quantities.

The real breakthrough came later that year when a four-piece band from Seattle, Washington, released their major label debut. The album was *Nevermind* and the band was Nirvana. Loosely dubbed as grunge rock or college rock (the latter a title R.E.M. had once been saddled with), they paraded a glorious combination of ragged pop melodies and thrashing, overwrought guitars. Seeing their pictures in magazines and record racks across the world it was hard not to draw comparisons with the anti-rock star stance of R.E.M. in their earliest days. Lank-haired, baggy-jumpered and workbooted—an entire generation of disgruntled youths now began to look the way Michael Stipe had when R.E.M. first terrorized the Athens club circuit.

Live at London's Borderline Club, 1991

> **"Corporate sponsorship is the way of the world, and it's futile to fight it, but I don't have to like it."**
> ***Mike Mills***

Of this new group of 'alternative' rock bands, many had taken their cues from the likes of Husker Dü, Black Flag and the other post-punk outfits that had shared cramped dressing rooms and roadside diners with R.E.M. And there weren't many from that era still around apart from R.E.M. They may have been still too quirky and too individual to fit conveniently into any musical bracket, but they nevertheless made for valid, if reluctant, role models.

The response on both sides of the Atlantic to *Out Of Time* finally completed the change in R.E.M's profile that had been building since *Document* and *Green*. Suddenly R.E.M. were living up to *Rolling Stone*'s slightly premature description as 'America's

Stipe, Mills and Berry collect an MTV Award, 1991.

MUSIC TELEVISION
VID
ANDGUN
ONTR

R.E.M.—in the spotlight

Hippest Band', while their decision not to tour frustrated Warner Brothers and served as a timely reminder that, best-selling album or not, R.E.M. were still determined to play by their own rules.

"The feedback I've gotten from that alone was more than anything else I've ever done. I was getting mail from countries that I couldn't even find on the map."
Michael Stipe on his fashion statements at an award ceremony

A promotional trip to Europe was hastily cancelled following the outbreak of the Gulf War, but was rescheduled for March, by which time *Out Of Time* had reached number one in the UK album charts. Despite their refusal to tour, the band couldn't resist the temptation of playing live and lined up two 'secret' gigs at London's Borderline Club under the name Bingo Hand Job. Not surprisingly, the 'secret' didn't last long and both shows were packed, with tickets changing hands outside for up to $200 (£80). As well as several songs from the new record, the band played acoustic versions of 'Disturbance At The

Heron House', 'World Leader Pretend', 'The One I Love', 'Pop Song '89', 'Fall On Me', the Troggs' 'Love Is All Around' and, joined by Billy Bragg, Suzanne Vega's 'Tom's Diner'—plus a handful of more obscure cover versions. Back in the US, the band appeared on the popular TV show *Saturday Night Live* and delivered a 60-minute performance for MTV's *Unplugged* series.

The lack of live shows meant that audiences had to make do with the videos and, demonstrating an admirable flair for the outrageous, Michael Stipe and producer Tarsem ensured that they would not be forgotten. 'Losing My Religion' came complete with a promo verging between the truly inspired and the wilfully pretentious. Using scenes from the Greek legend of Icarus, borrowing heavily from the British film maker Derek Jarman, and incorporating some amusing dance steps from Stipe, it stood out from the pack of identikit films on MTV. Stipe even broke his own rules and agreed to lip-synch for the first time ever, claiming (rather unbelievably) that "the first time I lip-synched for 'Losing My Religion', I fainted, I was so terrified". Outraged by the promo's combination of supposedly homoerotic imagery and religion the video was banned in Ireland.

It was the MTV Awards ceremony on September 5, 1991, that offered the final piece of evidence—if any was needed—of how popular R.E.M. had become. The awards were for videos only and 'Losing My Religion' was nominated for nine categories, winning six of them: Best Group, Best Alternative

Michael Stipe—look no hands!

WHITE HOUSE
STOP AIDS

Music Video, Best Video of the Year, and three technical categories. Peter Buck was conspicuous by his absence at the awards and only appeared at the party later. Mills and Berry were content to go quietly to the stage to collect each award, while Stipe took the opportunity to steal the show.

See T-shirt for details

Arriving on stage to collect the Best Video award, he appeared in a T-shirt bearing the single word "Rainforest"; for the Best Alternative Video award he returned wearing another with the legend "Love Knows No Colours". And for the final Best Video of the Year award he began with a T-shirt declaring "Wear A Condom", removed that to reveal another with the message "Choice", then "Alternative Energy Now", "The Right to Vote" and lastly "Handgun Control Now". Accused of pretension by some and of trivializing the issues in question and reducing them to the level of mere fashion statements, Stipe defended himself in *Rolling Stone* magazine: "If I was misunderstood or if people thought it trivialized any of the causes, then I'm very sorry. But the feedback I've gotten from that alone was more than anything else

Picking up their Grammy Award, 1992

I've ever done. I was getting mail from countries that I couldn't even find on the map."

Perhaps inspired by the positive reaction to 'Losing My Religion', Stipe and his C-00 film company set about making promos for future R.E.M. singles including 'Shiny Happy People', 'Radio Song' and album tracks 'Low', and 'Country Feedback', which along with 'Losing My Religion', 'Half A World Away' and 'Love Is All Around' (from their TV appearances) found their way on to another video collection *This Film Is On..*

With the band's popularity at a premium, I.R.S. released another compilation of earlier material in October 1991 (for the UK market only), under the title *The Best Of R.E.M.* This featured: 'Carnival Of Sorts', 'Radio Free Europe', 'Perfect Circle', 'Talk About The Passion', 'So. Central Rain', '(Don't Go Back To) Rockville', 'Pretty Persuasion', 'Green Grow The Rushes', 'Can't Get There From Here', 'Driver 8', 'Fall On Me', 'I Believe', 'Cuyahoga', 'The One I Love', 'Finest Worksong' and 'It's The End Of The World As We Know It (And I Feel Fine)'—16 songs in all. Not surprisingly, the album crashed into the UK Top 10 within weeks of its release, peaking at Number 7.

Michael Stipe—"That's me in the corner..."

R.E.M. in 1989

At the end of this, their most successful year to date, the band decided to pay tribute to one of their favourite bands by booking in at John Keane's Athens studio to record an album with the British Sixties group the Troggs. After R.E.M. had joked about recording an EP of Troggs covers, the band's manager Larry Page had contacted Jefferson Holt and studio time was booked. Laughingly titled *Athens Andover* (in honour of both bands' respective hometowns), the album was, at R.E.M.'s own admission, not to be taken seriously. It featured two

Michael Stipe—the film maker

new R.E.M. songs 'Nowhere Road' and 'I'm In Control' and a new set from the Troggs. Released in February 1992 the album attracted a degree of publicity but then sank without trace.

Cover versions

There were to be more collaborations around that time too. Billy Bragg also recorded his single 'You Woke Up My Neighbourhood' at John Keane's

> **"This is us taking a chance. People are either going to love it or freak out."**
> ***Bill Berry on*** **Out Of Time**

studio with backing vocals and guitar supplied by Stipe and Buck. Then the whole of R.E.M. returned to record a special fan club single titled 'Christmas Griping' along with a cover of UK punk band the Vibrators' 'Baby Baby', and further one-off recordings including a cover of Leonard Cohen's 'First We Take Manhattan'. Paradoxically, considering the number of cover versions the band had recorded or played live over the years, R.E.M. suddenly found their own material being covered by other artists. *Surprise Your Pig*—an album of R.E.M. songs recorded by 17 little-known bands was released through Staplegun Records the following summer.

With even greater irony, considering how many records they had sold in the mainstream markets, R.E.M. scooped the prestigious Grammy Awards for Best Alternative Album (and Best Video) in 1992. They attended the ceremony at New York's Radio City Hall on February 25, with Stipe bearing another message—"'White House Stop AIDS'—on his baseball cap. Justifiably proud, Peter Buck summed up the moment: "I can tell my mom I'm on the cover of every magazine in the world, but the Grammys are something she can grasp on to, something she can understand and tell her friends."

Fame at last.

Michael Stipe—towing the line

THE SIDEWINDER SLEEPS TONITE

The Nineties had brought long-overdue fame and wide recognition for R.E.M. But that sort of adulation always comes with another cost quite apart from hard work and marketing. "Almost all the fans I meet are pretty cool people; sensible people I wouldn't mind having a drink with," Peter Buck told *Q* magazine in 1993. "But once you're selling, like, nine million records—you're attracting people who aren't really fans. You start getting the psychos. I've had a couple of weird encounters, including a guy in New York who borrows money from people—and has lived with a woman—on the strength of being me! Poor bastard has to look like me—I feel sorry for him..."

And when checking into a New York hotel for the Grammy Awards, Bill Berry's mother had been shocked to find the band's personal assistant advising her to register under an assumed name to avoid any zealous R.E.M. fans that might scan the

***Michael Stipe*—'Man On The Moon'**

"Well, I would never have thought we'd last 13 years. But from the very beginning, we always said that R.E.M. was only the four of us, and it wasn't three of us with another guitar player and another bass player or something like that."

Peter Buck

hotel register in an attempt to locate the parents of their favourite drummer! Months later, the *Athens Banner-Herald* newspaper, ran a story about psychic Ian Bliss who claimed that R.E.M. were going to break up the following year... However reluctant the band may have been to assume the mantle of rock stars, it seemed that in some people's minds, R.E.M. were now the subjects of the same mass attention and adoration as other platinum-selling artists.

Such popularity did, however, have its benefits.

R.E.M. looking pensive

"America's Hippest Band."

R.E.M. in the front yard!

Out Of Time had been such a huge success that it allowed the band even greater freedom to follow whatever musical direction they chose. Still free from the restraints of touring, it was not long before they were back in John Keane's studio demoing new material with Scott Litt.

Back to four

One face that was noticeably absent from these sessions was that of second guitarist Peter Holsapple. He had played on the previous album and performed with them at live gigs and TV shows, but was still not considered an official member of the group. Allegedly unhappy with the wage he was being paid, and the fact that he was not involved in the band's songwriting, Holsapple considered himself

> **"Every record you make you get lost somewhere. This felt really strong right to the end."**
> *Peter Buck*

Michael Stipe and Pearl Jam's Eddie Vedder

in limbo—neither in R.E.M. or out. He finally opted out, later releasing an album with his former partner Chris Stamey from The dbs titled *Mavericks*.

Buck, Berry and Mills regrouped and as before, the new songs were thrashed out in an unconventional manner with the members swapping instruments, and with Buck relying once more on the mandolin instead of the guitar. "We'll have a folk rock orchestra album," Buck told *Spin* magazine journalist Jim Greer during the early sessions. "The stuff is all turning out different. We've got a bunch of weird kind of Arabic folk songs."

Michael Stipe joined the band once the demoing stage was over, and they flew to Daniel Lanois' studio in New Orleans, less than 10 months after the release of *Out Of Time*. From there on, the band and Scott Litt moved from studio to studio; apparently determined to turn the making of the new R.E.M. album into a cross-country adventure. From New Orleans they moved to Bearsville Studios in Woodstock, then Miami, and back to Athens where they recruited former Led Zeppelin bassist/keyboard

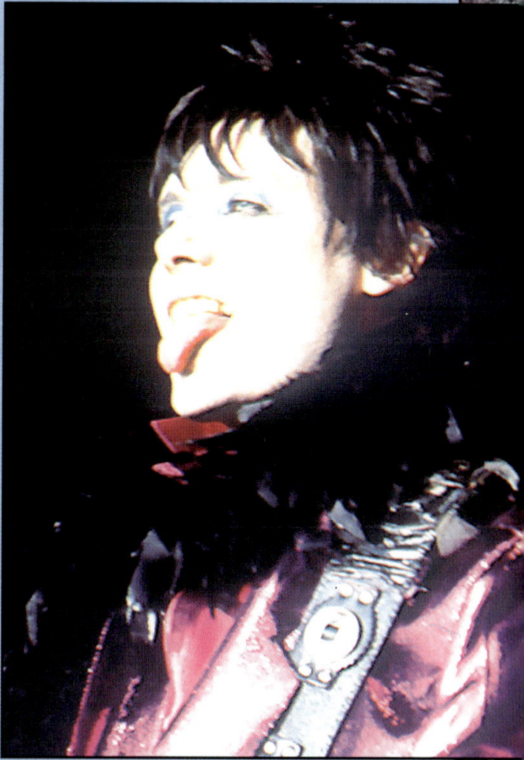

Manic Street Preacher Nicky Wire

player John Paul Jones to arrange the strings on four of the new songs. "I was really impressed with how melodic and non-saccharine his arrangements were," enthused Buck. They finally mixed the record at Bad Animals Studio, owned by the band Heart, in Seattle.

Automatic reaction

Titled *Automatic For The People* (a name inspired by an Athens soul food restaurant), the new R.E.M. album was released in October 1992. The 12 songs served up were: 'Drive', 'Try Not To Breathe', 'The Sidewinder Sleeps Tonite', 'Everybody Hurts', 'New Orleans Instrumental No. 1', 'Sweetness Follows', 'Monty Got A Raw Deal', 'Ignoreland', 'Star Me Kitten', 'Man On The Moon', 'Nightswimming' and 'Find The River'.

"We were planning to make a rock'n'roll record and go on the road, but they weren't rock'n'roll songs and I just didn't see the point," said Peter Buck. "When we actually wrote that stuff, there weren't going to be any drums on anything. There weren't drums on 'Drive', there weren't drums on 'Find The River', there weren't drums on 'Sidewinder' or 'Man On The Moon'. We sat down in a circle and worked

All join hands

up those songs the way the Beatles probably did. We'd say 'Here's the bridge', here's the intro, here's the outro.' So it was a real controlled record."

If *Out Of Time* had been a departure from the R.E.M. of old, then *Automatic For The People* was even more of a surprise. A reflective, at times mournful record, it seemed to combine the melancholy of early R.E.M.with the superior songwriting of *Out Of Time*. The upbeat, engagingly quirky 'The Sidewinder Sleeps Tonite', the charming 'Man On The Moon', and the hard-rock anti-government rant 'Ignoreland' offered the only respite from a stream of gentler, achingly tuneful songs. A skillful use of minor chords, string arrangements and some of Stipe's most haunting lyrics were displayed to strongest effect on 'Drive', 'Everybody Hurts' and 'Sweetness Follows'.

'Try Not To Breathe' read like a suicide note from an old man now tired of living. While the plaintive piano, strings and voice arrangement of 'Nightswimming' included some of the singer's most revealing lyrics. Although there was no outright mention of AIDS, many of the songs, especially 'Nightswimming' with its allusion to a better, safer time without, in Stipe's words "the fear of getting caught", had clearly been influenced by the disease.

Michael Stipe—playing up to the crowd

"I have a feeling that if one of us ever decided to quit, that the other three would have gone on, but with a different name."
Peter Buck

The music press were quick to pick up on the veiled references to AIDS in the album and, predictably, rumours began to circulate that Stipe

Stipe and Mills with U2's Adam Clayton and Larry Mullen, 1993

> **"I would like to make one record a year. We write enough songs but we've got to do press, we've got to do videos, we're going to be touring."**
> ***Peter Buck***

himself was a sufferer (his gauntness in recent videos being cited as evidence of a deteriorating health condition). One particularly grim outburst came in early in 1993 when Nicky Wire, bassist with outspoken Welsh rock band the Manic Street Preachers, referred to the rumours with the added insult of saying how he hoped Stipe had the disease! In typically contrary fashion the band refused to issue a direct rebuttal to such declarations, simply dismissing the rumours in subsequent interviews.

Within a week of its release *Automatic For The People* headed straight for the Number 2 spot in the US album charts and was only denied Number 1 by massively popular country artist Garth Brooks' *Ropin' The Wind*. It also reached Top 10s in Europe and Australia and eventually made Number 1 in the UK charts. It seemed as if R.E.M. had finally justified the *Sunday Observer*'s ambitious declaration that they were the biggest band in the world.

Out in front

In spite of this success they still seem reluctant members of rock's elite. Guarding his privacy to an even greater degree than before, Stipe remains the most elusive and intriguing member of the

R.E.M. at an MTV Special, 1993

band, often avoiding interviews and letting the others act as spokesmen for the group. There certainly seems to be some weight to the theory that Stipe's image as R.E.M.'s frontman is largely contrived, that much of the ambiguity surrounding his lyrics is deliberate, and that he enjoys playing up to this. R.E.M.'s audience have always been entertained by Stipe's mystique and there would almost be a sense of disappointment should he ever shatter the illusion and reveal himself to be the relatively ordinary, down to earth individual many suggest he actually is.

Yet Stipe's reclusive nature and regular changes of image meant that an R.E.M. sighting in 1993 was always newsworthy. Appearing on another MTV special in September 1993, Stipe looked fashionably thin and was crop-haired, sporting a beatnik's beret and matching goattee beard. Rejuvenated after so long off the road the band charged through a

Peter Buck and Neil Young, 1993

"You know what would be nice, if we just did the last three records live. You know, do *Out Of Time*, *Automatic For The People*, and the new one."
Peter Buck

ferocious version of 'Drive' and a searing, heartfelt 'Everybody Hurts'.

In the year following *Automatic For The People*, Stipe has become increasingly politically active, campaigning on behalf of some of the causes he first brought to the public's attention via his T-shirts at the MTV Awards. "I'm getting involved with an organisation called 'The Centre To Prevent Hand Gun Violence'," he told *Melody Maker*'s long-time R.E.M. authority Mat Smith. "I'm also working with 'Rock The Vote', some AIDS organisations, and some racial intolerance organisations." Stipe has also branched out into the film business, working on a forthcoming

Michael Stipe and Mike Mills at the MTV Awards, 1993

VIDEO
MUSIC
AWARDS
TALENT

Paying a visit to the 1993 MTV awards.

Oliver Stone movie *Desperation Angels*, described in typical Stipe-speak as "political", "very controversial", and "not funny".

Plans for the future

Another R.E.M. album is planned for release in the summer of 1994, with a tour to follow. Work on the record began in October 1993 in Acapulco, Mexico. "So far everything is electric guitar and loud," said Peter Buck, in December 1993. "I think we'll be going for a more lively feel. We'll be working with Scott Litt again. We wanna capture a more live performance. I think *Automatic For The People* is the best thing

"The success of Nirvana proves that kids like hard rock and they don't have to have their rock stars dressed like their grandmothers in teased hair and leather pants."

Peter Buck

R.E.M. admire the view.

we've ever done. But we've done that now, so we need to do something else. I was in Sicily and all my Italian friends were going 'Peter just throw away that acoustic guitar and mandolin. Just throw them away'!

"We just said 'Okay, everyone write rock'n'roll songs'—and it was great because we all met and we

"I love touring, and everyone else does too to different degrees."
Mike Mills

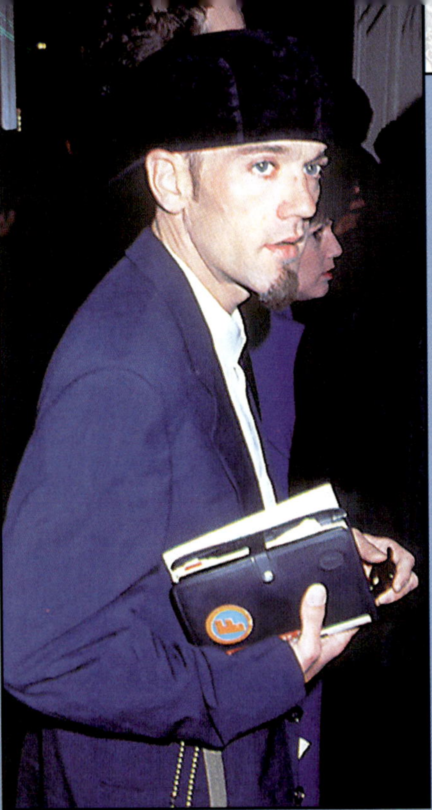

Michael Stipe—making an entrance

"I've done my share of whatever there is to do, but I just spent my entire life trying to get out of situations where I had to follow other people's rules or orders, getting out of school and all that, and I just couldn't imagine harnessing myself to a drug dealer's schedule."

Peter Buck

each had, like, 10 songs. Bill, Mike and I. And then Michael had a bunch of lyrics and we put down about 24. We'd do about four a day, without even rehearsing them, just put them down and do them. So ideally, I'd like to do a really long record next time, maybe 18–20 songs. And make it noisy—I'm ready for that. We are a rock'n'roll band and it just feels kind of logical to turn the amps up and get the drum kit out and bash away," insisted Buck.

"I know we're going to tour after the next album," claimed Mike Mills to *Q* magazine. "Everyone says you can sell 'x' records and make 'x' millions of dollars. That's not the reason to do anything. We play all the time, nine or 10 times last year, but free or unannounced, for 40 minutes. I like that."

"I'd love to play some of the Eastern Bloc countries, or whatever used to be the Eastern Bloc countries," said Buck. "We've never played South America. I certainly don't want to play soccer stadiums so we'll have to figure out how to do it. It would be fun to do it really impractically and tour and play 1,000-seat halls. You know what would be nice? If we just did the last three records live. Do *Automatic*

Michael Stipe—learning to fly!

Michael Stipe—down among the crowds

Michael Stipe—an angry young man

For The People, *Out Of Time* and the new one. I mean the responsibility is to make whatever we do... to do it as well as we can, and not be condescending to the audience."

In the fall of 1994, the group released a new album, *Monster*, which reaffirmed their position as arguably the biggest act in the world when it topped the charts on both sides of the Atlantic. *Monster* marked the band's return to a harder-edged rock sound, compared to *Automatic for the People*.

Even in the late 1980s, Michael Stipe had mentioned a 'real and raw' album they were planning, but massive international stardom had forced them to delay the project in favour of a more

"Almost all the fans I meet are pretty cool people. They're intelligent and tend to think about things a bit more than your average rock'n'roll fans."
Peter Buck

Michael Stipe and beard!

fashionably acoustic approach. *Monster* lived up to its name, becoming the third R.E.M. album in succession to enter the British album charts at Number One, and their first to do so in the States. Its sales in Britain during its first week of release exceeded 200,000 copies, more than any other album had sold in one week for five years, since the hugely popular *But Seriously* by Phil Collins.

Double platinum in Britain, triple platinum in the States—things were still going rather well....

R.E.M. are clearly not going to sit on their success and watch their egos grow. So perhaps it's worth leaving the final word to the inimitable Mr Stipe: "I'm one-fourth of an incredibly successful pop group. I sit around, people come up to me, talk to me, photograph me... I like my life."

"So far everything is electric guitar and loud."
Peter Buck

DISCOGRAPHY

Album title	*US/UK CD catalogue numbers*	*Released*	*Chart placing*
Murmur	US: IRS 70014	Apr 1983	—
	UK: A&M CDMID-129	Apr 1983	—
Reckoning	US: IRS 70044	Apr 1984	27
	UK: IRS 7045	Apr 1984	91
Fables Of The Reconstruction	US: IRS MC5592	Jun 1985	28
	UK: IRS IRLD 19016	Jul 1985	35
Life's Rich Pageant	US: IRS MC5783	Jul 1986	21
	UK: IRS DMIRG1014	Jul 1986	43
Dead Letter Office	US: Not advised	Apr 1987	52
	UK: IRS 70054	Apr 1987	60
Document	US: IRS MC42059	Sep 1987	10
	UK: IRS DMIRG 1025	Sep 1987	28
Eponymous	US: IRS MC6252	Oct 1988	44
	UK: IRS DMIRG 1038	Oct 1988	69
Green	US: Warner 25795-2	Nov 1988	15
	UK: WEA 9257952	Nov 1988	27
The Collection (Fables... Life's Rich Pageant, Document, Dead Letter Office, Eponymous)			
	US: Not advised	Aug 1990	-
	UK: Not advised	Aug 1990	-
Out Of Time	US: Warner 26496-2	Mar 1991	1
	UK: Warner 7599-26496-2	Mar 1991	1
Best Of...	US: No release		-
	UK: IRS DMIRH1	Aug 1991	7
Automatic For The People	US: Warner 45055-2	Oct 1992	2
	UK: WEA 9362-4055-2	Oct 1992	1
Monster	US: Warner 45740	Sep 1994	1
	UK: Warner 9362457632	Sep 1994	1
EP			
Chronic Town	US: IRS AM 70054	Apr 1987 (CD reissue)	-
	UK: IRS CDA 70054	Apr 1987 (CD with **Dead Letter Office**)	-

CHRONOLOGY

December 6, 1956 Peter Lawrence Buck born in Oakland, California.
July 31, 1958 William Thomas Berry born in Duluth, Minnesota.
December 17, 1958 Michael Edward Mills born in Orange County, California.
January 4, 1960 John Michael Stipe born in Decatur, Georgia.
April 5 1980 R.E.M. (playing under the name of Twisted Kites) make their first public appearance at a friend's birthday party in Athens, Georgia.
May 15 1980 R.E.M. make their first headline appearance at Tyrone's Club, Athens, Georgia.
December 1980 R.E.M. support the Police at the Fox Theatre, Atlanta.
April 1981 R.E.M. record their first demo tape with producer Mitch Easter.
May 1982 R.E.M. release their debut EP *Chronic Town*.
April 1983 R.E.M. release their debut album *Murmur*, recorded in Athens with producer Mitch Easter.
July 1983 R.E.M. release 'Radio Free Europe' as a single.
August 1983 R.E.M. support the Police at New York's Shea Stadium.
January 1984 Peter Buck, Bill Berry and Mike Mills form a side-project band, the Hindu Love Gods, with singer Warren Zevon.
April 1984 R.E.M. release their second album *Reckoning*, recorded in Athens with producer Mitch Easter.
December 1984 R.E.M. contribute the song 'Windout' to the soundtrack for the movie *Bachelor Party*.
June 1985 R.E.M. release their third album *Fables Of The Reconstruction*, recorded in London with Producer Joe Boyd.
September 1986 R.E.M. release their fourth album, *Life's Rich Pageant*, recorded in Indiana, with producer Don Gehman.
October 1986 The single 'Fall On Me' reaches no 94 in the US charts.
January 1987 R.E.M. begin a US tour.
May 1987 R.E.M. release a compilation album of B-sides and out-takes, entitled *Dead Letter Office*.
September 1987 R.E.M. release their fifth album *Document*, recorded in Nashville, with producer Scott Litt.
October 1987 R.E.M. play their first UK tour for three years.
December 1987 The single 'The One I Love' reaches Number 9 in the US charts.
June 1988 R.E.M. sign to Warner Brothers.
October 1988 I.R.S. release a best of R.E.M. compilation entitled *Eponymous*.
November 1988 R.E.M. release their sixth album *Green*, recorded in Memphis with producer Scott Litt.
June 1989 The single 'Orange Crush' reaches Number 28 in the UK singles chart. R.E.M. make their debut appearance on the UK TV show *Top of the Pops*.
August 1989 Michael Stipe forms his own film company C-100 and releases the live R.E.M. video *Tourfilm*.
January1990 R.E.M. release a collection of their promo videos, *Pop Screen*.
March 1991 R.E.M. release their sixth album, *Out Of TIme*, recorded in Woodstock and Athens, with producer Scott Litt.
May 1991– *Out Of Time* reaches Number 1 in the US charts.
September 1991 R.E.M. win six awards at the MTV Award.
October 1991 I.R.S. release a compilation album *The Best Of R.E.M.*.
February 1992 R.E.M. receive a Grammy Award for Best Alternative Album.
October 1992 R.E.M. release their seventh album *Automatic For The People*.
September 1994 R.E.M. release their eighth album *Monster*

INDEX

Picture Acknowledgements

Photographs reproduced by kind permission of **London Features International**; **Pictorial Press**/Hashimoto-NGL,/Jeffrey Mayer,/Paul Natkin,/Vinnie Zuffante; **Redferns**/Mike Cameron,/Michel Linssen,/Ebet Roberts; **Retna Pictures**/Edie Baskin,/Chris Carroll,/Steve Double,/Amando Gallo,/Karl Grant,/Patrick Quigley,/Aaron Rappaport,/Steve Rapport,/Gary Sershoff,/Ben de Soto,/Loayne Stambler,/Chris Taylor; **Rex Features**/Bleddyn Butcher,/L Cottrell,/Dave Hogan,/James Kelly,/L.G.I.,/Stills,/Richard Young; **Syndicated International Network**/Peter Anderson,/Andrew Catlin,/Jane Huntingdon,/Tony Mott,/Leo Regan,/Zbysiu Rodak,/Roy Tee